# Dancing on the Narrow Ridge: Superintendents' Ethical Decision-Making

by

**Keith D. Walker**

**&**

**J. Kent Donlevy**

**Copyright © 2010, 2013 Keith D. Walker**

**All Rights Reserved**

**Published by**

Turning Point
GLOBAL

Calgary, Saskatoon, Kingston, Wellington, NZ

**ISBN: 978-1-300-35723-0**

# Abstract

This monograph describes approaches to ethical decision-making used by educational decision-makers, based on findings from survey responses (n=136) and interviewee data (n=20). The approaches are organized into four categories: relativism, utilitarianism, reflectivism, and deontologism. Following the presentation of each category, a critique of each approach is provided from the viewpoint of Martin Buber's concepts of "I-Thou" and "I-It," while positioning the decision-makers' choices of approach on what Buber calls the paradox of the "narrow ridge." Lastly, this monograph suggests how educational decision-makers might best approach ethical decision-making taking into account Buber's concepts.

# Table of Contents

# Introduction

> I have occasionally descibed my standpoint to friends as the *narrow ridge*. . . . I wanted by this to express that I did not rest on the broad upland of a system that includes a series of sure statements about the absolute, but on a narrow rocky ridge between the gulfs where there is no sureness of expressible knowledge but the certainty of meeting what remains undisclosed.[1]

Martin Buber's concept of the *narrow ridge* may be interpreted as meaning that the individual decision-maker finds that ethical decision-making is not based merely upon what is right or wrong, true or false, but rather decisions that are forged within a state of paradox where there is a unity of ostensible opposites. For some, Buber's sense that there may be a unity of the contraries and mystery in dialogue (two truths brought together) may be a relief, to others the notion may generate despair, and to others this proposition may signal a call to defend a better way with more robust ethical doctrines. Buber said,

[1] Buber, 2002, p. 218

> According to the logical conception of truth only one of two contraries can be true, but in the reality of life as one lives it they are inseparable. The person who makes a decision knows that his deciding is no self-delusion; the person who has acted knows that he was and is in the hands of God. The unity of the contraries is the mystery at the innermost core of the dialogue.[2]

It is on this *narrow ridge* that superintendents and assistant superintendents of education[3] stand in dealing with ethical decision-making. For some, they are torn not just in the choices they make, but more particularly in articulating the ethical warrant for their choices. Philosopher J. L. Mackie[4] suggested that

> A moral or ethical statement may assert that some particular action is right or wrong; or that some actions of certain kinds are so; it may offer a distinction between good and bad characters or dispositions; or it may propound some

[2] Buber, 1948, p. 17

[3] As our readers will be aware: chief educational officers or chief executive officers in Ontario and Saskatchewan are often referred to as "Directors;" most other jurisdictions refer to these leaders as "Chief Superintendents."

[4] 1977, p. 9

> principle from which more detailed judgements of these sorts might be inferred - for example that we ought always aim at the general happiness or try to minimise the total suffering of all sentient beings, or ....... that it is right and proper for everyone to look after himself. All such statements express first order ethical judgements of different degrees of generality.[5]

This monograph uses research involving a sample of educational leaders in Canada and looks both quantitatively and qualitatively at the ethical warrants which they claim to use to justify their ethical decisions: providing a critique of the same from a Buberian perpspective. Lastly, we offer Buber's approach to ethics as an alternative understanding for ethical decision-making. Particularly, this monograph will: provide the rationale for our research; state the methods, philosophical perspective, and methodology applied to interpreting the data; categorize the participants' responses into four ethical frames of thought with a brief critique after each; and offer our perspective on how superintendents might live ethically,

[5] (Retrieved from: http://www.bola.biz/ethics/whatis.html)

if not comfortably, on the *narrow ridge* of ethical decision-making.

# The Rationale

The rationale for this research and subsequent findings represented in this monograph responds to the need for academic understanding of the topic and the professional needs of educational leaders in the field.

Despite the many texts and conceptual treatments, the field of educational administration and leadership has only rarely seen evidence of actual descriptive and empirical research on the nature of ethical decision-making.[6] It is still true today that, as Kowalski (1995) said, "there have been only a handful of studies examining this administrative position. Even more troublesome is the fact that we know surprisingly little about contemporary conditions of practice and about the individuals who now hold these jobs" (p. viii). Fullan (2003) said, "the single key for unlocking the resources and capacities that we will need is an enlarged conception of the moral imperative of school leadership . . . it's time for school leadership to come of age" (p. 80). This monograph addresses several aspects of these calls for research and capacity building by considering the specific ethical warrants that a sample of

[6] Enns, 1981, pp. 1-8; Gronn, 1987, pp. 106, 107; Leithwood & Musella, 1991, p. viii; Begley, 1999; Begley & Leonard, 1999; Walker & Shakotko, 1999; Walker, 1995a; 1995b; 1994

superintendents used in their decision-making and providing our analyses of these.

The usual research approaches in applied ethics are oriented toward observation of behaviours or the analysis of participant responses to preconceived situations or ethical challenges. This monograph complements these approaches through a methodology that allowed the leaders to voice their own meanings and understanding with respect to the nature of ethical decision-making as well as measuring the responses of leaders to predetermined ethical orientation statements. Toffler (1986), Bird and Waters (1987, 1989), and Jackall (1988) are representative of the early researchers who sought to develop first hand reports of the nature of ethical decision-making amongst administrators. Again, here we provide the reader with some insight into superintendents' ethical grounds for decision-making, as they speak for themselves and attempt to go beyond superficial descriptions ("begreifen," in Ladd, 1957) to look, rather, at leaders' understandings from an inside perspective ("verstehen"). Bird and Waters (1987) alerted those researching in the ethical domain that leaders will not likely be systematic or traditional in their use of ethical language. This means that the descriptions, to follow, do not fall neatly or systematically into tradition schools of ethics but we have organized our findings using conventional and *a priori* categories or frames.

Jackall (1988), in his attempt to report on the first hand moral experiences of corporate managers, said "[m]anagers may disagree with some of the broader interpretations of their experiences suggested here. We have tried, however, to capture the complexities, ambiguities, and anxieties of their world" (p. vii). This expression captures our project efforts as well. It was noted by Walker and Donlevy (2009, 2006); Lennick and Kiel (2005); Walker (1994, 1995a, 1995b), Enomoto and Kramer (2007); Parsons (2001); Beckner (2003); Maxcy (2002); Nash, (1996); Sergiovanni (1996); Starratt (2004, 2003, 1994); Ziebay and Soltis (2005); and Bottery (1993) educational leaders are sometimes reluctant to discuss, with candor and clarity, their ethical dispositions and, further, that it may be that some are "ethically mute." That is, they may not have the language capacity or expressive vocabulary to articulate their moral viewpoints. The common isolation of educational leaders from those peers who might benefit from ethical conversation may be another reason to support the view that some educational leaders may not have had or taken the opportunity to acquire the language of ethical discourse and certain dialogical competences.

In sum, this monograph responds to the academy's need to access first-hand voices from the field and to provide those in the field with an understanding that they are not alone in their anxiety and reticence to discuss ethical decision-making by seeing their peers' views while offering a language to express their own understandings. Hopefully, we provide an opportunity for leaders to reflect upon the difficult, complex, and often-ambiguous nature of ethical decision-making.

# Methods, Methodology, and Philosophical Perspective

This study employed both quantitative and qualitative methods in delving into the depths of educational leaders' ethical decision-making. Quantitatively, 136 educational leaders, drawn from both from the public and Catholic school systems, were surveyed: one third were superintendents of schools (sometimes called chief superintendents, chief educational officers, directors or superintendents of education, depending on jurisdiction) and two thirds were assistant superintendents (see survey items in Appendix B). Twenty participants, all male superintendents, were interviewed twice each to discover, explore, elaborate, and interpret their warrants used in ethical decision-making. More than half of the interviewed superintendents were from rural districts and the superintendents represented smaller school systems, ranging from 10 schools to over 60 schools. In total, the 20 superintendents interviewed had 5,161 instructional staff and 86,513 students in their jurisdictions. The data were collected, coded, and analyzed for common themes and for quotations which were exemplars of the variety of those themes. The philosophical perspective and applied methodology was objectivist grounded theory, which as Charmez (2000) stated,

> accepts the positivistic assumption of an external world that can be described, analyzed, explained, and predicted: truth, but with a small *t*. That is, objectivist grounded theory is modifiable as conditions change. It assumes that different observers will discover this world and describe it in similar ways. (p. 524)

Ten natural or *a priori* principles were presented in the form of ethical statements to measure the extent of superintendents' agreement or disagreement with those principles, together with descriptive items (commonly associated with various ethical schools) (see Appendix A). The interview data were grouped into four general ethical frames: teleological, deontological, relativistic, and reflectivistic. These four ethical frames were considered to be discrete constructs by means of construct validity; however, the factorial procedures administered to the survey item responses suggested that these orientations are somewhat "messy." The participants enhanced or challenged the boundaries of these four ethical orientations as they were provided with latitude to give their own interpretations and expressions.

It is to the frames and the data, with brief commentaries on each frame, that we now turn. The basic pattern we have followed is to present quantitative data (from survey), followed, within frames, by themes emerging from narratives of leaders and our commentary.

# Four Ethical Frames, Examples, and Commentary

Superintendents were asked to speak for themselves through interviews and open-ended questions. Their orientations toward particular ethical theories were linked to the implicit and explicit ethical grounds for decision-making. While these ethical orientations are complex and the analysis was reductionistic, the process served to provide a sense of the extent of adoption and the meanings associated with the orientations from the perspectives of superintendents. Most of these educational leaders tended to possess complex, multiple-ethical orientations, but exhibited tendencies toward one or two particular orientations. They generally viewed their decision-making as dynamic and dependent on the types of problems and pressures presented by their varied contexts. It is fair to say that four ethical frames emerged from the quantitative and qualitative data provided by the participants in this study: teleology (utilitarianism), deontology (duty), relativism, and reflectivism. We provide exemplars from their data in each frame next in this monograph.

## Teleological Frame

The teleological fame is rooted in the understanding that ends or goals are used to judge the rightness or wrongness of actions. Simply put, the ends are seen to justify the means employed to achieve those ends. However, in ethics, the choosing of the ends must be consistent with the nature of the entity making the choice such that for humans, the end is, in utilitarianism, happiness. While clearly not the dominant theory of ethics-in-use for superintendents, teleology sometimes referred to as act or rule utilitarianism, was certainly utilized.

Sixty percent of leaders did not agree with the commonly expressed utilitarian principle that the most ethical decisions were those that result in the greatest good for the greatest number. Fifty-seven percent of leaders disagreed with the concept that in dilemma situations, the optimal choice produces the best social consequences. Only 31% of leaders disagreed or strongly disagreed with the view that a leader should first ask which alternative is consistent with the overall welfare and happiness of those in the organization when making a difficult decision. A relatively large group of respondents (22%) indicated their neutrality. Eighty-one percent disagreed that the rightness of an action was best determined by projecting the degree of happiness resulting from the action and 69% of the leaders disagreed that decisions were right in proportion to their tendency to promote happiness. So general happiness, harmony, or utility was not a strong ethical compulsion for these leaders. We suspect that if survey items were framed in less abstract fashion, to focus on particular group happiness or utility (i.e., students), then the response might have been different.

Utilitarians are often depicted as considering the efficacy of a policy based on the greatest good resulting as a consequence of a decision or action. In this study, 56% of leaders did not agree that consequences were the primary criteria for determination of rightness or wrongness. This indicates that these superintendents were less inclined to teleological, utilitarian, or consequentialist orientations than to other criteria.

This said, 71% of leaders still agreed that the maximization of short- and long-term benefits for the school community should be the first consideration of educational policy-makers. This indicates that superintendents agreed with the utilitarian concept of benefit maximization, over time, as a decision-making criterion. Seventy-nine percent of respondents also agreed that honesty was a moral rule because of its promotion of social harmony.

Four utilitarian orientations emerged from the data: best interests of the "kids" grounds; securing educational goals; long-term interest grounds; and well-being of stakeholders' grounds.

## (1) Best Interests of the "Kids"

In the interviews with superintendents, there was no mistaking the assertion that the children were the primary stakeholders in most school jurisdictions. Some interviewees expressed their conviction that there were high and low stake issues in their educational deliberations. The decisions having to do with "children and their benefits – doing the very basic things for children" were considered much more important than "the political games played" by some leaders.

Another leader expressed this same orientation when he said, "you stick to the straight line – you do the best you can for the 'kids' and take your lumps." This perspective that the benefit of the "kids" was held as a higher order value than the welfare of the administrator was expressed by the following two statements:

> You are dealing with people's lives and you've got to make sure that you are considering their best interests and the kids. The kids' best interests are the most important and you have to remind yourself of this when dealing with these issues. The ethics of doing things for kids . . . Is this the best thing for the kids in the classroom? I have developed the Board in such a way that they use this as their ethical basis for decision-making. Are we making the best decision for the kids that we serve? As a group we formulated goals and a motto for doing things for children. You might call this 'the best interests of the children ethics.'

However, the concept of "the best interests of the kids" was considered by some to be "too simplistic" and, by others, as vulnerable to misuse. These superintendents indicated that this "best of for the kids" grounds for decision-making had been passed off for lots of things of questionable benefit to kids. One interviewee commented that,

> As apple pie and corny as it may sound, my position in budgeting is based on doing our very best for kids. The easiest way of dealing with the budget is cutting teachers, but this cuts at the very core of what we are doing. So I don't cut back on teachers. That's the biggest ethical thing I tell them. Over a few years this is a great place to save money but that it strikes at the core of what we are trying to accomplish in this system. I could really not do my job and sell the kids in the system down the river . . . . I think it is unethical to sell the kids down the river.

This ground was also used to rationalize or justify the use of unacceptable means wherein the ends were shown to be beneficial for the children. One leader, for example, said,

> What differentiates the right from the wrong is based on one's value system. I begin to weigh the benefit for the kids. Sometimes if I bend [my value system] it's because I might see that the effort will benefit the kid. There is a bit of manipulation but I don't struggle with this

> too much if I can rationalize it to myself [in this way].

This leader found himself able to justify the means, manipulation, by way of the *goodness* of the results with respect to benefiting a child or the children.

## Securing Educational Goals

The utilitarian basis of decision-making which placed securing high quality education for the community was commonly expressed during the interviews. One superintendent expressed this in a particularly interesting fashion. He said,

> [My] bottom line is to provide the best quality of education for the people in our communities and within our jurisdiction - that's where I begin and [in]everything I do – I think you would find a string attached to that base.

When asked to clarify, the superintendent explained that everything decided in his jurisdiction must be linked, as if literally tied by a string, to the educational goals which, in turn, are rooted in the delivery of quality education.

## Long-term Interests

Two leaders explained their thought processes when deliberating over difficult long-term interest decisions. They described their thinking as follows:

> Every decision I make I ask – is it for the good of the schools? Where I might have to make a decision, constraints like the fallout in the schools or the ultimate harm to the system come into play. It might be the right thing to do – but the overall health of the school system is really important.

> Our long-term plan really helps, when things get tough, because you can always come back and focus on the plan rather than focus on the immediate concern. We felt it was the right thing to do then and it helps to keep things in focus.

Sometimes the superintendents would combine principles such as in the example below. Here the school system leader asserted that the best interest of students, over time, will differentiate the relative quality of his decision-making. He was strongly in favour of those decisions which were more long-term and understood that short-term gains, or losses, might need to be forfeited, or suffered, to attain long-term benefits for students.

> Sometimes you have to look at a long-term good as well as the short term good. That is a critical point when you are dealing in the best interests of the children. On certain occasions, I would be accused of making decisions that weren't in the best interests of children. I say – judge me five years from now. There is a big difference between short and long-term decision criteria.

Another interviewee suggested that the long-run consequences of politically motivated decisions were antithetical to the educational goal-oriented decisions which he favoured. He said,

> It is not prudent in the long run to make political decisions. The right or prudent

> thing is to aim for that vision and goal. If that is the principle, it is not right to be political. The principle is the content or goal towards which you are headed and prudence is the process of getting there in the most apolitical manner possible.

Long-term interests must always be considered not only for the best interests of the stakeholders but also the institution as it is that which has, in general, the greatest stake in perpetuity.

## Well-being of Stakeholders

This ground for decision-making provided for a social-focus with respect to the ethics of superintendents. This utilitarian doctrine characteristically highlights the school systems' responsibility to all stakeholders. For some, this was a safeguard against self-interest on the part of professional educators or elected trustees. It also provided assurance that each child, regardless of background or abilities, would be appropriately educated. Rule utilitarianism holds that we should establish and maintain rules whose general observance maximizes happiness for all and that this yields the greatest total amount of satisfaction for those concerned. Some utilitarian-oriented superintendents claimed that the well-being of the community was their main consideration in choice making. As one leader stated,

> Well, the first thing that goes through my mind is . . . Okay how is that going to impact or affect the community? Who am I going to hear from first, and you know, what is going to be the message coming back? One, the first things is the impact or effect.

Another superintendent posed a similar question, in the context of a difficult staff problem,

> You have to make decisions based on how can we deal with this without hurting a lot of people? You have the student to protect, you have the other staff to protect, and you have the rights of the individual.

The estimation of decision impact on all the stakeholders was critical to some superintendents. One said he thought "the critical thing [was] to assess the impact of the decision and [that] you must assess the impact of the decision on all the people in the organization." While it was not a common suggestion, a few described their decision-making in a fashion that closely approximated the classical utilitarian perspective of promoting happiness for the greatest number. An example of this was presented by a superintendent, who said,

> You can have really nice school facilities but if those suckers aren't any good in the classroom, and I am talking about teachers and administrators, then she breaks down. As long as the teachers are good and the parents are happy with the instruction their kids are getting then you can have a high mill- rate and the people will pay. I really promote the band – 'cause people in our system will vote based on how well they like the band on Sunday afternoon.

The rule utilitarian stipulates that there are valid, non-universal moral *rules* or *beliefs* that guide our human decisions toward maximizing the good in society. Some superintendents felt that policies, rules, and decisions were justified only on the basis of "bringing about the greatest amount of good to the members of the learning community." The need to consider the common good of the stakeholders was expressed, but in several interviews, the superintendents struggled when asked to differentiate the notions of the public good or interest, the common good, and the benefit of those within the organization. For some, the utilitarian principles were utilized to govern their decision processes, and for others, the principles provided criteria for determining the rightness or wrongness of decisions. The former use is exemplified by the superintendent's comment that,

> I talk about options. I touch bases with other people who might be affected – we have to understand the consequences of each of these options. You are influenced. What does it do to the whole system, how will it be seen in that particular community – when it come right down to it – Is it best for education? By doing what I am doing, is this the best way to serve the people?

This utilitarian orientation also provided a bottom line kind of decision-making ground for some leaders. When discussing tough budget decisions, one superintendent said,

> [I like to ask] how does this decision affect the people involved, what kinds of messages and things are communicated? The bottom line is – how much of a

> difference does it make to everyone and how big a difference?

A negative expression of this ethic is the so-called "Silver Rule," or "Do No Harm Ethic." The essential teleological frame for the utilitarian views of the best interests of the kids, securing educational goals, long-term interest grounds, or the well-being of stakeholders rests clearly upon a calculation of what are the best long-term interests of a particular group or the institution. There are many difficulties with this approach, not the least of which is which group's interests is referred to in the calculation, to ethical decision-making, as we shall see.

## Commentary on the Teleological Frame

Act or Rule Utilitarianism exemplifies the 'I-It" relationship as it seeks what is in the best interests of the majority or the desirable end which results from an act. In either event, there is a calculus involved which is entirely ends-oriented. Put starkly, it is an ethical orientation which allows the decision-maker to act in a sterile, calculating, analytical fashion by seeing "the other" as a pawn in achieving an end. The decision-maker is a moral calculator, making a non-personal decision and justifying it, no matter how uncomfortable it may be, as the "right" decision given the objective at hand. This orientation does not provide guidance regarding who constitutes the group entitled to have its best interests served by the decision-maker. Thus, in deciding upon the end as "the best interests of children" one can sacrifice the interests of teachers, parents, or the school system. Without the precondition of knowing which group's interests to address, one can sacrifice the well-being of stakeholders, based upon any criteria of the day, and so the ephemeral, or politically motivated, trade-offs continue. In effect, the prioritization of the best "ends" can change with the political wind or the succession of a new school board. Utilitarianism's principles will not provide the ends to be achieved, only the calculation with which to achieve the ends. Once again, decision-makers find themselves on the narrow ridge where one side of the call may be for the 'best interests of the children," while on the other side may be the call to "long term interests of the school system." On the basis of utilitarianism alone, one cannot decide how to determine which group to prefer and thus which of the ends to choose as, paradoxically, both may seem of equal importance and thus determinative.

# Deontological Frame

The Deontological frame is, contrary to the teleological position, based on the understanding that adherence to an ethical principle is of the utmost significance in ethical decision-making, no matter what the cost nor to whom that cost may be imputed. It is, to use colloquial parlance, a "do the right thing" approach to decision-making. The deontological ethical orientation was generally affirmed by the survey respondents.

During interviews, superintendents provided elaborations and enhanced the descriptions of the deontological grounds (or “Duty Ethics”) used in their everyday decision-making. Responses indicated that 87% of leaders agreed with the “kingdom of ends ideal” that people should be treated as ends not means to ends. This is a fundamental Kantian formulation of respect of persons which states we have a duty to not “use” people; instead, persons are inherently valuable and have their worth without account of or use of utility to serve some other end. Similarly, 96% of leaders agreed that leaders should always treat people as subjects of value rather than instruments for accomplishing particular purposes: 66% strongly agreed with this statement. Sixty-one percent of leaders agreed that an egalitarian expression of fairness gave force to social norms while over two-thirds of the leaders agreed, or strongly agreed, that leaders weigh their primary duties in order to help sort out ethical dilemmas. Sixty-five percent of the leaders agreed with the classical deontological statement that one ought to act in such a way that the principle of one's act could become a universal law. Ninety-five percent of leaders agreed, or strongly agreed, that respect for other persons constituted the most basic, rational criterion for moral decision-making. Of course, this indicated a strong orientation amongst leaders to the deontological concept of respect for persons. Eighty-two percent of leaders agreed, or strongly agreed, with the consistency or precedence principle that "what was just for any person in a similar situation" should be the basis upon which subsequent decisions were considered and 88% of leaders indicated that honesty was a moral imperative because it constituted a basic human duty.

Deontological theories are often presented as determining decisions to be "right," to the extent these conform to relevant principles of duty. These deontological ethical theories are often negatively defined as non-consequentialist and tend to focus on obligations or duties imposed by self, society, or theological belief. In the descriptions to follow, superintendents provided deontological warrants for decision-making that were expressed as: self-evident duties; rules of obligation; the reversibility principle; impartiality and dignity of persons; and retrospective obligations.

## Self-evident Duty

Like the act deontologist, a number of the superintendents saw no necessity for appealing to pre-established principles or rules to establish their obligations to their school system stakeholders or their governing Boards. Some viewed their decision-making as a straightforward matter of determining the rightness or wrongness of a decision and having the necessary organizational or positional power and/or courage to act accordingly. On one hand, there were superintendents who felt more autonomous than other leaders in their organizations and, on the other hand, some felt more closely bound to the rules and policies established by their Boards than they supposed, other members of the organization did. However, with respect to the everyday decision-making, and in the large area of discretionary decision-making, many chose to develop their intuitive abilities to approximate the doctrine of act deontology. Some superintendents held that ethical values could be directly and immediately apprehended. Of these, a few argued that every situation merited its own unique attention. These were not easily differentiated from the situationalist grounds, which will be discussed later under relativistic frame.

While most leaders claimed to have a set of rules or principles by which they made most of their decisions, some leaders expressed the belief that they simply knew the right thing to do in particular circumstances. They held that this rightness was self-evident. The doctrine of act deontology is commonly described as a form of duty-based ethic which judges actions as right, based on their degree of conformity to rationally or intuitively determined obligations. A classic expression of act deontology was espoused by one of the superintendents:

> You have your rules and your policy book and then you have your day-to-day operations. You don't quote to people – this is what the policy says or this is what the board says! You deal with the situation – don't hide behind the policy. You can't operate in a people organization using guidelines that way. It is too legalistic an approach. System policies and rules are not self-justifying – they can't just be laid on.

> You are always writing your policy. Every situation has a different twist. Usually we find that we are ahead of the policy formulation. We usually update the policy. We are living somewhere between what we wrote and what we are now writing as new policies.

The self-evident ground for ethical warrant seems to appeal to the "institutional nature" of decision-making which is bound by policies and local conventions, be they political or social.

## Rules of Obligation

As indicated, most superintendents claimed to base their decision-making on rules or principles. For some, these rules were a means to an end. One superintendent explained his view that codes were to be servants of leaders who often need help interiorizing the ideals expressed by the deontologist orientation. He said,

> We certainly have a code of ethics for our organization and we have basically approved that code. I guess from my perspective I see it more from an

> individualistic point of view rather than organizational point of view. I am a Rotarian – and I really like our four way test (i.e., is it the truth? Is it fair to all concerned? Will it build good will and better friendships? Will it be beneficial to all concerned?). [We noted that this ethical rubric from the 1930s contains both deontological (1 & 2) and teleological (3 & 4) rules.] Those particular questions are something that I sort of want to govern my personal life by. So, I guess in answer to the question, I would say that each individual . . . needs to have a personal, ethical sort of philosophy of what they really believe and you think of that on a regular basis. I like the whole concept of the four-way test; it makes you think. So, like the code of ethics, it is simply a reminder of some of the things that we should be doing. I think these all fall into the whole idea of treating people with respect and making sure that you are fair and that you are truthful.

One of the most notable features of rule deontologism is its adherence to the principles of consistency (or universality). Like Kant's autonomous individual, a number of leaders said they used good reasoning to determine whether decision alternatives were in conflict with their set of *a priori* moral values. A key doctrine of Kantian deontology (formalism) relates to the concept of respect for others. The concept was expressed in a variety of ways by superintendents, ranging from safeguarding people from harm, abuse, or exploitative experiences to the more positive approaches of care giving, imputing dignity and worth to people, and being sensitive to people's needs and individual differences. One superintendent expressed this obligation when he said, "[t]he need for respect for others has not changed – it needs to be recognized and upheld in the school. Parents expect this."

## The Reversibility Principle (the Golden Rule)

The reversibility principle or the Golden Rule (do unto others as you would have them do unto you) was used by many superintendents as a grounds for decision-making. The Golden Rule has also been formulated (more recently) as "do unto others as they would have you do unto them." This is said to be a more respectful articulation of the age-old rule. One educational leader combined this principle with the self-sobering perception of his role as a model for others to follow. He wished to be safe to follow and yet wanted to empathize with others in his decision-making. This view held to the old ideal that a leader must be far enough ahead of his followers, but accessible enough to ensure that the last person in his or her entourage can touch the leader. He said, "I need to look at myself in the mirror . . . I need to walk in the other person's shoes. I have to remember the fact that I am a role model." The Golden Rule and respect for persons rule were elaborated as ethical grounds by another superintendent, as follows:

> In my personal life, I live by the Golden Rule a lot. I don't want to treat other people in a way that I don't want to be treated myself. I want to be consistent in my regular life and my professional life. Treat people in a way that I would like to be treated myself - with dignity and respect.

Of the 20 leaders interviewed, only one had developed a generic philosophy statement with respect to an ethical grounds or moral orientation for his school system. He expressed his organization's deontological grounds in the following manner,

> I would think the ethical issues are embedded inside other things. I tend to try to think of ethical concerns as fundamental, human issues. We have a policy developed as a part of the philosophy statement called the "duty of care." In it we suggest that everyone in the organization has the right to [receive] care. The three components to the duty of care are: due regard for the human individual, due diligence, and hard work as one carries out their professional obligations, and thirdly, due process or fair treatment. We argue that these [ethical] principles should underlie everything we do – should underlie instructional practice, personnel practice and so on. When I talk about what are fundamental driving forces, I find it very easy to say – where does our duty of care fit in here and are we in fact living up to the expectations that we say we believe.

This philosophical statement was strongly duty-oriented and seemed to be used by the superintendent quite frequently, even during the course of the interview. He claimed it was a real help in his administrative deliberations. When asked to what extent these duties of care were known to his staff and the community, he expressed the need for renewing and reviewing them with the organizations' stakeholders but cited a couple of examples wherein school principals, to his surprise, had justified their debate on a particular ethical issues with this statement.

## Impartiality and Dignity of Persons

The central idea of contractarianism is the provision of single grounding principles for decision-makers. Egalitarians stress the concept of fairness while libertarians emphasized the notion of freedom. The superintendents in this population seemed to emphasize both sets of principles. Their contracts were moral obligations which seemingly provided criteria for moral decision-making. Human equality and human dignity were apparently sought by these leaders through conscious efforts to ensure impartiality and by the establishment of procedures for determining various entitlements. Libertarian theories are sometimes characterized by their attention to economic distribution and for their advocacy of distinctive procedures and mechanisms to ensure that individual rights are recognized. The emphasis on contractarian grounds was especially evident by the frequent reference in the surveys and interviews to concepts of equality and fairness. The concepts of justice, fair play, due regard, and due process were all interrelated as expressions of the egalitarian and libertarian ideals. Most expressions of these principles seemed to be blended.

Like the egalitarian theorists, superintendents tended to support the thesis that individual differences should not bear significant preferential consideration for the decision-maker. Superintendents were concerned in their decision-making to ensure that the distribution of both the burdens and the benefits of their organization were characterized by being just and fair. Impartiality or independent objective judgment were conceptual instruments used by leaders to ensure that they were being fair to all their stakeholders. This was similar to what Rawls (1971, pp. 20, 48, 49) called the "veil of ignorance." An example of this veil of ignorance was crudely expressed by one leader, who indicated that,

> If you can somehow sit back and imagine what it looks like to people who don't have the information – if you can somehow sit back and say – okay what kinds of things will be perceived by others – when you do that – I don't think any of us will come to situations without biases – so you need to

> be prepared to justify your biases and fight for your positions.

Several superintendents reviewed their school system's procedures for hiring administrators as examples of formal sets of assurances that every aspirant was fairly and duly given potential access to the open position. A superintendent added that,

> you want to have a process that is objective so that right choices are not preempted by non-relevant constraints. If you have, for example, made up your mind ahead of time on who should get the next principal's position, then what is the point of the process? You cannot rule out the possibility of factors that are built into the selection process. The outcome will be predictable but it is not certain . . . It is fair process . . . people are given opportunity to move ahead. Such a process takes away the subjectiveness.

Another example of this procedural justice was expressed with respect to dismissals. One superintendent said,

> dealing with something people-oriented – you've got to treat people fairly and correctly. If you run up against that situation where there is a problem – you can slip very quickly to the thought of dismissal when there are at least seven or eight intermediate steps that ought to be considered [first]. You wonder if that person was out of here we'd be better off. But you just can't do this.

Superintendents not only expressed contractarian grounds by the processes undertaken to ensure fairness but also indicated their commitment to these grounds by ensuring that certain collective entitlements were upheld within their jurisdictions even at the expense of expediency. Two urban superintendents exemplified this when they stated the following,

> As the superintendent of education, I have purposefully sent the strongest staff into the poorest school, to my own risk, because of what's going to happen. The reason [is that] I want them to find out some of the solutions to what we can do better on a day-to-day [basis]. Can't do that if you don't send the best people to where the greatest challenge is. And what

it creates, of course, is [a situation] where the wealthier people are chasing you – the easiest way is to send the better teachers [to them] and then they don't chase you.

When you come to money - It is easy when times are good to solve problems with money. You can buy somebody out or give something to a community to shut them up; it's easy to give the teacher who grates on the nerves of the principal something, but it is not right. It is inequitable. Those are the kinds of decisions that eventually create the biggest issues. That's why you need to educate people about why equity is important. Gender equity and Native rights are important. We have to balance what we give each school. Those can be just day-to-day decisions. You don't start putting in computers where people are the most vocal. The decisions that you can get away with are the one's that you should be the most suspicious of and be the most careful to make the right decision on. Some will say – well if it has to be cut back ten percent then everybody has to cut back

> that much. That doesn't sound to me like a good decision – it certainly isn't just.

Another superintendent added to this contractarian grounding through his attribution of the equality of persons, rather than merely the equality of distribution. He said that he was,

> . . . Careful to be mindful that you are working with people - every job is equally important. There is just no job in this school that isn't as important as any other job and you take any one of them out and it is going to be less than it was before. I think that is important to remember that all of us, whether it happens to be the janitor or the board chairman or the superintendent– you have to be civil to people. And that again, in tying this whole thing back to ethics is how you treat people.

One senior educational leader expressed his district's practical resolution to these fairness and dignity obligations by the following example,

> We try to stress with all employees that everybody has to have a sense of ownership. We

> have institutes and workshops for all employees in the system – not just teachers. The ground is leveling out. This speaks a lot of messages. These significant soft items are what builds the heart of real community – these are not the hard rules. You have to make decisions in this soft and gray area. You have to stand for justice and the individual.

The concept of treating people with dignity was a reoccurring theme amongst these executives. One said,

> Treating people as if they count when you make a decision – you do so leaving people with their dignity. It is unprofessional to strip someone of their dignity. Give people some options; let them maintain their dignity and let them make the decision. Giving a person a chance to maintain their dignity even when they are going through a tough time and when they are not competent to behave professionally and you know it and they know it. You give them a chance for an honourable retreat. You've got to give them the information and you've got to go through all of the steps. I will be recommending to the Board that your

> contract be terminated; I'll give you a week to think about it. They may not choose a dignity-saving option . . . I can only give them the opportunity.

A final example of how the grounds of contractarian justice were expressed in the decision-making of leaders was vividly portrayed by the situation described by one of the interviewees. Notice that the grounds of fair treatment were linked to the concepts of natural justice (expressed as due process) and the unconditional dignity owed to every person. The reader will also note the ethically reinforcing effect of this decision-making on the other stakeholders in this superintendent's organization. He described his decision-making as follows:

> For example, when a teacher was charged with sexual assault I wanted to treat the person fairly. It had nothing to do with whether the person was innocent or guilty. If it had gone the other way we would have been out several weeks' pay but we would have done the right thing. This had a great effect on the other staff because it showed that we are willing to at least give people a chance and not jump on them immediately; to be supportive to people

> during the due process. It was we who were involved in getting this guy charged. I was the one who called in the police because it was something that we could not clear up without them. So it was our decision because we owed it to the kids but we also owed him due process and some kind of dignity. This person has now become a great asset to us.

## Retrospective Obligations

One of the most obvious ethical grounds for decision-making amongst superintendents was referred to as the law of origins:

> The law of origins asks: what are we here for? This is what you have to ask as a fundamental starting place for your ethical decision-making framework. What is best for 'kids' and school together with common sense? When you talk in terms of what is best for 'kids' you are always dealing in the right arena of consideration. If I was wanting an epitaph for my work, as a superintendent, I would want to be

> evaluated as one who lives the law of origins and used his common sense.

One other said that he guessed “you would have to take it right back to why we exist. That’s got to be the underlying reason. In fact you’ve got to remind yourself of that all of the time.” These were paternalistic and retrospective grounds for decision-making which might be superficially distinguished from the teleological “best interests of the 'kids’ orientation” by their subtle mission or professional obligation frame of reference. The superintendents espousing this as an important basis with which to justify their decisions seemed to feel that it was their duty to safeguard the original purposes and mandates for which they were hired and why the school district, itself, was established. This mandate orientation may be described as sustaining the public and professional trust. One superintendent's comments exemplify these perspectives. He said,

> What you have to do is to base your decisions on whose rights you are protecting and your mission. Your mission is for the children and so on; so, therefore, you are going to do everything you can to protect the rights of that child. Also you are bound to your staff, the laws of the

> land; so you have some obligations to protect staff.

A final example of this retrospective grounds was provided by a superintendent who suggested that crises often bring the taken-for-granted assumptions of the organization to the surface and provide an opportunity for leaders, and others, to reaffirm their professional obligations to their educational *raison d'être*. As he stated,

> I think in the long haul people will respect you for making the hard decisions. They will look at the good things as well as the bad things that have happened. Crises clarify assumptions and cause people to reflect on what they are in the business of doing and being.

The leaders' responses within the deontological frame demonstrate that self-evident duties, rules of obligation, the reversibility principle, impartiality and dignity, and retrospective obligations make up a large part of the ethical tool box used by those leaders. However, the deontological approach is problematic for various reasons, not the least of which is that the decision-maker, although publically appearing to acting ethically, may fail to be authentic to her or his self.

## Commentary on the Deontological Category

Kantian deontology with its emphasis on categorical imperatives (acting such that the act can become a universal law, and treat others as ends in themselves and not means), appear to offer objective guidance to ethical decision-making. However, the first type of formulation is predicated upon honoring the rational, the calculative in human relations. The second focus is upon the *ought* which derives from rationality and universal laws. As Friedman (1960) stated, "Thus Kant's imperative [treating others as ends] is essentially subjective (the isolated individual) and objective (universal reason) . . . . In Kant, the *ought* of reason is separated from the *is* of impulse" (p. 200). Kant's approach is quite different from Buber who suggested that the other is indeed an end in herself or himself, but that is so because of the distinct nature of the *I-Thou* relationship and the act of the authentic *I* (in the sense of being present, in a concrete sense) being created in the action of that relationship. In that regard, and in real life experience, the decision-maker is indeed on the narrow ridge between the *ought* and the *is* which coexist in the paradox of experiencing being. Norms are important and as Buber (2002) stated,

> No responsible person remains a stranger to norms. But the command inherent in a genuine norm never becomes a maxim and the fulfillment of it never a habit. Any command that a great character takes to himself in the course of his development does not act in him as part of his consciousness . . . [it] remains latent in a basic layer of his substance until it reveals itself to him in a concrete way. What it has to tell him is revealed in whenever a situation arises which demands of him a solution of which till then he had no idea. Even the most concrete universal norm will at times be recognized only in a very special situation. (p. 135)

Self-evident duty and rules of obligation amount to general rationalizations for action but are not singular to the individual or the situation. Is it any wonder then that such an approach may cause some disquiet at the core of the decision-makers? Both contractarianism and the law of origins offer little more, as the former is a clear statement of the *I-It* relationship of means to an end, albeit with a *quid pro quo*; while the latter reflects upon past obligations to determine action.

Is this too intellectual an analysis of decision-making, which many claim is determined by the attitudes and values of the culture within which the decisions are being made? After all, is not ethical decision-making relative? It is to the educational leaders' responses to this question that we now turn.

# Relativistic Frame

The relativistic frame typically denies that there is a singular authoritative template of ethical values, for all people for all time. Rather a particular value which appears to be ethical in nature must be seen in light of any number of factors in order to determine if it applies or, indeed, has any significance to a particular case. Those operating in this frame argue that no single standard of behaviour – and hence ethical value – applies to all people at all times. Therefore, what the individual or group accepts as an ethical value is particular to that single instance, situation, or individual or group. One would not say that what has been accepted is good or bad in a universal sense.

In our study, 85% of leaders did not agree that morality was to be conceived of as a matter of taste not reason, moreover, the findings indicated that 79% of respondents thought it was unreasonable to act in their own interests; yet, 46% of superintendents believed that people are not innately constrained to act in the best interests of others. Forty-four percent of leaders did not agree that what was good, right, or virtuous was dependent on community sentiment. However, 43% of leaders did so agree. Forty-six percent did not agree that "morals constantly change and that astute administrators adjust to these changes in their decision-making." Beyond, or beneath, these bare statistics are the meanings which educational leaders ascribed to their ethical warrants. Indeed, their discrete statements point to some interesting grounds for ethical decision-making.

In this third frame, emerging from the interviews with leaders, the ethical orientation of relativism was expressed through: emotions (personal preference); egoism (self-interest); cultural relativism (community sentiment); simple relativism (extra-rational grounds); and context relativism (situational sources). The survey item orientations (scales) and the interviewee descriptions elaborate the superintendents' regard for relativistic doctrines as ethical warrant for their decision-making.

## Emotions: Personal Preferences

The emotivist doctrine (Ayer, 1952) suggested that nothing said in moral terms should be regarded as either true or false. This form of relativism prescribed that sentimental idiosyncrasies are the only ethical grounds for decision-making. Morality is more a matter of taste rather than of reason. For some educational leaders the activity of decision-making consisted of gathering as much information as possible and simply making the best decision on the basis of rational considerations. Their desire was to either treat "ethical" decisions as undifferentiated from any other kind of decision or to discount the so-called validity of ethical opinions as "too fuzzy for me." These leaders felt that, while there was a place for feeling or sentiment in their deliberations, their positions required them to render objective, scientific, or empirical judgments on all issues brought to them.

## Egoism: Self-interest

Although, as above noted, the majority of the respondents thought it was unreasonable to act in their own interests; yet, almost half of them believed that people are not innately constrained to act in the best interests of others. This paradoxical position is exemplified by the following quotations:

> [S]elf interest is bad because a person, like myself, is in a position of public trust – we are trusted and have the opportunity to affect people's lives . . . when you get away from that – when you don't do what is in the public interest – but do what is in your

> self interest – you are no longer a professional and you no longer deserve the authority, the responsibility or the job.

> I guess the worldview I think of is that of survival. I didn't make the world, I am just trying to get through it like everybody else. I will accept some responsibility for working for change but that is all I can do. Survival is what it is all about. I guess that guides me.

The latter quotation points to the seemingly uncontrollable survival risks perceived to be inherent in administrative work. Some participants thought that such risks, to themselves, could be either reduced or escalated by their ethical actions.

In response to asking what constituted unethical behaviour for him, one superintendent responded,

> Not doing your job to the best of your ability – to save your hide you might slip something by the Board on a certain issue – here you verge on being unethical and I think all of us at times are guilty of that. There are times when you start ducking and

> diving to save yourself and times when you let things go by at a Board table that you know are wrong but given the mechanics and political situation at the time it's not strategically worth fighting for because you are going to lose another battle down the Board meeting agenda or you lose a much much larger item. The ones I would let slide are the ones I don't find too unethical because the bottom line isn't as important. I think a person is unethical – if you don't give it your best on the job at all times. [For me] unethical means lying and cheating, doing really bad things. Ethics is a continuum, and superintendents slide all the time. I think there is a point on the continuum that you don't go over. Along the line there are varying shades of gray.

The above leaves the reader with the impression that in determining what is unethical one is on a sliding scale of what is necessary in a situation to either achieve a goal or to survive politically, with the determining factor being the potential egregiousness of the unethical act, which in turn is determined by the how one feels at the time.

## Cultural Relativism: Community Sentiment

Educational leaders were split in their views regarding the mutability of ethical grounds. One leader provided his view that ethics were sometimes socially mediated. He said,

> I would like to say that ethics are socially mediated and that people decide what is ethical and what is not ethical. It is not clear in any one issue or situation. In my experience it is not always easy to predict how an issue will fly – it depends on moods and who has had a bad day.

It is a common sentiment that determining if the "bubble on the level" is centered, in an ethical sense, is best determined by the collective. It appears that a significant number of the participants determined the acceptability of the collective or community test as being determined by both the seriousness of the case and the seriousness of the impact of the decision on those involved. The decision may be the same in cases, but the process of determination is thus relative.

## Simple Relativism: Extra-rational Warrants

Simple subjectivism may be described as a form of decision-making which finds its source in the extra-rational realm. Ideals or opinions are based on our feelings. For example, when a person says a moral behaviour is good or bad – they mean to say that they approve or disapprove of the particular action. A number of superintendents provided examples of such a view. The first of these was a clearly extra-rational perspective,

> If it doesn't feel right or it bothers my stomach or I am having some second thoughts then I better rethink the darn thing. It is doing something to my system. This works for me – personal, intuitive uncomfortability with a particular decision or action that you do which makes me go back and rethink it. Why am I doing this? Is it being done for the right reasons? Why am I struggling with this? If this happens then I go back – if I am comfortable and it feels okay then it tends to be a more correct kind of thing.

Two other superintendents exemplified this subjectivist perspective when they said,

> I think that being ethical has a lot to do with being able to live with yourself. I think it relates to how you feel inside. It is very subjective . . . based on a value system and feelings. If you are rubbing your value system wrong, then you need to do one of two things: justify it and try to live with it or change in order to maintain the dignity of your value system and continue to let it guide you. Value systems can be used as guidance or you can just ignore it. I think it is a good guidance tool but it is very hard to verbalize . . . it is so personal.

> You go through life struggling with feelings and values – it is a constant struggle of life. You are confirming, denying, or ignoring your basic value system as you go through life. I guess that is what it is all about. You've got a system and you go through life and you struggle with that value system and the value system translates how you act and how you do the job of the director. So it is a personal thing.

The above quotations are interesting as they focus upon and are indicative of the inner self of the decision maker seeking to "live with" the decision *ex post facto*. It reflects an assessment of the self's conscience not during the decision-making process but after the fact.

## Contextual Relativism: Situational Warrants

There is an ethic that decision-making is context specific. In the following examples, superintendents described what might be termed the situationalist grounds for decision-making. One leader said,

> Every situation is unique. Every person and circumstance is different. There is always a little kink; every student problem is different. There are some surface similarities and through experience you begin to learn what to do and what not to do.

The quotation below provided a near classic example of Machiavellianism when superintendent explained his approach to decision-making. He said that most decisions have,

> The shading of grays . . . if you did everything on principles you'd get into all sorts of troubles. You do what you can in as many cases as you can. Most leaders are virtuous in my opinion. You don't worry about whether manipulation takes place 'cause you have manipulated to bring about positive growth. The question is not whether you manipulated but to what end do you do it. [When] you find yourself in the business of manipulating for the wrong reasons then you better get the hell out fast. Intent and motive is really important.

The relativist frame contains ethical decision-making warrants based upon emotions, egoism, cultural, simplicity, and context. All five of these subcategories reflect the decision maker seeking justification for her or his decisions both in the public sense, as with contextual or cultural relativism, and in her or his own inner psychological world.

## Commentary on the Relativist Frame

For many respondents, what is evident in this category is the idea that acting ethically is related to being in a position to act. Survival, in an administrative sense, must be considered in the ethical analysis. The analysis is also self-referential. There is a strong sense of self but little of the other (i.e., students, members of the school board or teachers). This type of ethical decision-making stresses the "I" in the "I-It" relationship as, by definition, the "It" has significance only in terms of what is experienced by the "I" in terms of using the experience, and thus others, for an end. It is not mutual, or relational, the action has no meaning in and of itself without the end sought and is, therefore, a subject-object type of relationship. Friedman (1960, p. 58) described Buber's position on this matter, when he said, "man can live continually and securely in the world of it. If he only lives in this world, however, he is not man, for 'all real living is meeting' (p. 58). What is missing in the ethical analysis of many of the respondents is the experience of deciding from the experience of being in relationship with the other, be they students, staff, parents , business community, board members, or teachers. What is missing is the "I-Thou" relationship which demands immediacy, concreteness, and relationship in and for itself. The superintendent who steps outside of the subject-object relationship with "the other" finds wholeness in relationship as the response is "I-Thou." It is in that relationship, when engaged in making an ethical decision, that one finds that "no deception penetrates here; here is the cradle of the real life" (Buber, 1958, p. 12). Here then on the narrow ridge with pragmatism, with all its political calculations, and morality on either side, the decision-maker is whole.

## Reflectivistic Frame

For the purposes of this monograph, the reflectivist frame is composed of a variety of ethical thought involving core character values; *practical wisdom* and the *golden mean*; religion based criteria; and natural law criteria in ethical deliberation and discernments. This frame is based upon the pre-modern form of understanding ethics as based on reason, human inclination, natural and special revelation, reflection and virtue. The character of a person manifest through habit of exhibiting reasoned actions, consistent with apprehension of natural laws, the best of human inclinations and/or divine design. The key is the decision-maker deliberating upon action in terms of those core ethical values.

Fifty-four percent of superintendents said their moral philosophy stipulated that they should endeavour to do what was right from God's perspective. Similarly, 53% of the superintendents indicated that they agreed that the best test of right and wrong was whether or not a supreme being would approve of a particular decision. In accord with the former statements, 51% of leaders agreed that right moral action was measured by one's keeping obligations to a higher power. Another statement on the survey referred to the appropriateness of the Ten Commandments or the Sermon on the Mount as key ethical considerations in decision-making. Interestingly, a large number of respondents (34%) were neutral and 48% agreed with this affirmation of a revelationalist or divine law ethic.

Eighty-four percent of leaders agreed that honesty was a universal moral rule because of its intrinsic goodness and 65% of superintendents agreed or strongly agreed with the natural law perspective that morally right decisions were those consistent with natural and reasoned insight.

The principle of avoiding harm to others was affirmed by 92% of leaders. Eighty-eight percent of educational leaders agreed that they should never lie or cheat. Half of the leaders agreed that the needs of another human being always place those of us with resources in positions of moral obligation. Ninety percent of superintendents agreed that educational leaders must scrupulously guard their ability to make independent ethical judgment. Ninety-three percent of leaders affirmed their obligations to accept responsibility for the foreseeable consequences of both their decisions or non-decisions; while 79% of respondents agreed that superintendents must always endeavour to act beyond reproach and avoid every the appearance of impropriety in deference to the public trust. In the affirming opinion of 94% of educational leaders, there is a special obligation to respect the democratic processes of decision-making and avoid concealment of information. Finally, 69% of the superintendents agreed that a person or organization always has a responsibility to make reparation for wrongful acts.

Character-centered, wisdom-centered, religion-centered, and natural principles provide the headings for the reflectivist orientations described in this section.

## Character-centered

The superintendents expressed their view that there were certain core values related to behaviours and attitudes which were considered to be "ethical." Leaders were considered to be virtuous when possessing these attitudes, and vicious when behaving against certain ethical values. These ethical values were considered to be "people-friendly" and, negatively, as vices to be avoided. Heroes were characterized as those whose behaviours and attitudes had approximated these ideals, and villains were those leaders operating out of self-interest and who had transgressed one or more of these values. We suggest that these person-centered and virtue-oriented values are directly related to the schools of ethics that we have collectively entitled "reflectivist doctrines."

These reflectivist doctrines of ethics were characterized as giving primary consideration to character-centered judgments, based on either revelation or naturally derived insights. These theories focus on the kind of persons that superintendents thought they ought to be, as decision-makers. Plato's intuitive theory of ethics may be described as focusing on virtue derived from, or reflective of, both insight and consensus. Unlike Plato's claims that conflicts were incompatible with a proper concept of virtue, superintendents were often confronted with dilemmic situations where the conflict was between two or more values. Similar to Plato's vision of moral absolutes, which served to define and universalize "the Good," many leaders claimed to have intuited a sense of "the good." This good for leaders tended to be towards both effectiveness (contrary to Plato but in keeping with Homer and the Sophists) as well as towards certain excellences (as with Plato). Homer was criticized by Plato (in *The Republic*) for his rather relativistic approach to role virtues (i.e., "might is right") and the pragmatism of the sophists (i.e., "what works is right"). "The Good," in this view, seemed to be understood in terms of a smoothly running, ordered educational organization; one full of happy, productive and client-centered people. While justice was the guiding virtue for Plato, it would seem that attitudes of caring and respect, fairness, professionalism, stewardship (respect for resources), integrity, loyalty, honesty and citizenship were the virtues held in high esteem by these respondents. One leader expressed this high, but difficult to articulate view of virtues as follows:

> A superintendent must be a person of good character but [when the] question is asked – Who decides [what is good character]? I suppose jurisprudence and practice will tell us . . . if you are a good character now, then whatever criteria you are using continues to apply.

The character-centered ground explained above, seems to beg the question of what is a good habit – yet it was acceptable by many leaders as sufficient warrant for ethical decision-making. Thus, relativism tends to seeps into this warrant.

## Wisdom-centered

Aristotle was the chief proponent of an ethical school which argued for a kind of understanding grounded in the logic of both science and wisdom. He saw ethics as a *branch of politics* and viewed individuals as necessarily acting as members of communities. Many respondents had trouble with the juxtaposition of politics and their professional roles. They felt these were two conflicting paradigms and some had established these as strictly dichotomous perspectives. For Aristotle, training in virtuous conduct and good judgment involved learning to avoid two extremes: one was the vice of excess and the other was the vice of defect. Integrity was the balancing of various virtues in the context of internal and external demands. While the quandaries described by these leaders went beyond Aristotle's extremes of excess and defect, they did exhibit the leaders' desire to weigh the political and ethical merits, and demerits, of contending values, divided interests, means, and ends conflicts and frustrated acts of rightness. As with Aristotle's reflectivist view, the wisdom of a leader to intellectually and morally sort through these quandaries was considered praiseworthy. Like Aristotle, many leaders contended that to be ethical they had to learn on the job and to mature with the administrative challenges. However, superintendents were often conscious of the lack of formal training received for the work they were engaged in. One leader described the challenges of his work and his preparation for it when he said,

> Most of what we do – nobody has ever trained you for – this is a mess. By mess I mean being a superintendent [at this time in history]. It has always been a mess. My wife attended a meeting that I thought was only in a minor way challenging. When we got home she asked me – 'why the hell do you like doing that job?' You can't get trained for this business – most of it is on the job training. A lot of it is survival and for me there was some mentorship by someone I thought did a good job.

Almost all of the superintendents who were interviewed spoke of their need to give themselves daily, solitary time to think and reflect on the challenges. Interestingly, the majority did most of this reflecting in their cars. A number of urban superintendents recalled the sense of loss that they had experienced when coming from rural jurisdictions which had demanded a lot of travel time or being "office bound." This travel time was used to mull over the tough choices and to prepare for the events of the day. Other superintendents used conferences or their homes as places of retreat. Some leaders admitted to doing most of their reflecting late at night. The same superintendent provided an example of the typical rural superintendent's explanation of reflective time. He said,

> I think a lot in the car - last year I drove 25,000 miles or 50 eight-hour days . . . that's where most of it comes. Some comes laying awake at night – not able to go to sleep when a lot of things start piling up – that's not good thinking time but it happens. Frankly, this is a real problem. You get so busy doing that you kinda' forget the focus and the philosophical stuff. So every once in awhile, you deliberately see that happening and you kinda' step back and refocus again. There used to be seasons but not anymore.

Another superintendent responded to the quest for thinking time in the following manner,

> I don't do this often enough. I am basically a very solitary person. I drive a great deal. I do a great deal – trying out ideas with other people in the business that you respect. I have to replenish myself, personally, and consolidate my personal values in my

> personal life so that I feel really good about myself when I come into a situation so I have something to give somebody else or to give to my board or my system. If my personal life is in pretty good shape then I can come in and I am fairly confident and that kind of exudes from me. People will follow you if you show that you've got it all together. So I need time, personally, to make sure my personal life is on track. In some ways my career went up the ladder very quickly and my professional decisions were getting away ahead of my personal life – so I kind of opted out of what I considered the fast track and let my personal life catch up.

Apparently able educational leaders were characterized in a fashion similar to Aristotle's person of practical wisdom, as one having the ability to see what should be done in particular circumstances. Superintendents tended to view ethics in practical terms, as did Aristotle. The virtuous superintendent works according to ethical reason in the context of a community of educators. Peer and associate collegiality were highly valued by most superintendents.

Formal ethical descriptions were not the strong suit of superintendents; but they, nonetheless, ascribed to the practical importance of being ethical in the reflectivist sense. As one superintendent said,

> My way would be who you are as a person . . . you are one part of this organization, you work with other people and you have got to be ethical, whatever that means, you have got to be that. I don't even know if you can define it, but you still have to practice it even if you can't define it and one does practice it or maybe one doesn't practice it, but I think you know when you are practicing it.

The wisdom spoken of above seems to flow from life's experience (particularly on the job experience), reflectivity on those experiences, and the formation of habits which engender ethical behaviour and ethical decision-making in the respondents.

## Religion-centered

Expressions of the religious-moral reflectivist orientation were quite conspicuous in superintendents' ethical thinking. Most references to theistic or other religious worldviews were made by Catholic school superintendents. However, for one public school administrator, the notion of ethics and religion were inseparable concepts. This superintendent provided one of the few examples of responses utilizing philosophical literature. He said,

> I don't think you can divorce the religion and the ethics stuff. You can't ground your ethics in communicative rationality itself – it has to be grounded in something more. This moral relativism stuff and some of this post-modernist stuff – I have real problems with it. Habermas tries to ground ethics in communicative rationality, but I would guess that he will have to end up grounding it in Lutheranism. How the hell do you talk about ethics without talking about the Judeo-Christian concepts?

These religious groundings were most often evidenced in one of four ways. The most obvious of these were the superintendents' references to religious codes or expectations. Some of these codes were attributed to humans and some to God. These codes were generally characterized as prescriptive and normative grounds for behaviour and attitudes. One Catholic superintendent put it this way:

> At the local school level, we have got the Code of Canon Law [to] which we must adhere. This Code describes the responsibilities of the school to the church, and in particular to the parish priest, . . . I have a board that I work for, but also I work for the Bishop and so do my principals. They work for this Board but they also work for the parish priest . . . so when push comes to shove in the faith area, here, it is the parish priest who calls the shots and it is not the school board or the superintendent of schools.

Another leader, working with a Catholic school system, described a more paradigmatic view of religious-reflectivist grounds for decision-making as he elaborated on the freedom and general "Gospel" orientation embedded within his system. His emphasis seemed to underline religious aspects of the life of the administrator within the context of a faith community. This concept was somewhat similar to the community of friends promoted by Aristotle. Notice the superintendent's last sentence wherein he referred to the idealistic features of these ethical grounds. He said,

> In the Catholic system you are able to live your faith in your work totally and talk

> freely in your work. It is just a beautiful feeling, a freedom there. You don't have to worry about what you can say. No, you have a faith dimension . . . there that you can express in your work that is beautiful. But, at the same time, you have the added responsibility of that faith dimension because our Faith has clearly articulated what they want us to do. At times it makes you think that you have to jump tall buildings in a single bound, you know, because the bottom line that you can always hear is that "we wouldn't expect that kind of treatment in the Catholic school system" or "you are not following the Gospel message." So we are always caught between trying to reach beyond our reach and yet at the same time keep our feet on the earth.

One leader, from a religiously oriented school system, noted the counter-cultural mandate inherent in his community's ethic. Contrary to the promotion of conformity or syncretism, this superintendent suggested that being different was a Catholic virtue. He indicated this in these words,

> this is a counter-message – you see one of the problems we have in Catholic

> education is a substantial part of our Christian message which is counter to what is being said in society. So we are in counter-culture work.

It was, however, possible to be at odds within the Faith community while acting in ethical conformity to the world outside this community, as one superintendent describes,

> Your whole life is to be an example of our own personal faith or a faith expression. In Catholic schools there are certain areas where you can come into conflict with the community. Once you come into those conflict areas, that obviously are not acceptable to the Faith community, then you have to make some decisions. You have to weigh that out against the right of individual expression. You have got the right of individual expression but the moment you become a teacher, the moment you become an administrator, you have to be that Christ-like model in the community. It doesn't mean that you don't make mistakes, but you have to be that. Where you blatantly just refuse to follow the teachings of the church, you are in trouble.

The traditional religious virtues of faith, hope and love were expressed by a few of the separate school system superintendents as displayed below:

> We want to develop the faith of our community. We are really concerned with the faith life of the teacher. We need to maintain a strong commitment or fidelity to our mandate. If we don't, then it isn't right, and Catholic schools come to an end. I want us to communicate in such a way that they learn two things and only two: God loves them and they were made in His image, you are a perfect human being – He loves you. And second, no matter what you do in this world no matter how you mess up – God will forgive you. God will welcome you home and you will never be alone. The love part links Christ in as we realize that He sent his only Son here – that's powerful. Second, that Son died for our sins so we can be forgiven. There are only two things to walk away with in a Catholic education. If they could learn those two things and our system could actualize those two things it would be wonderful.

The most subtle expressions of religious reflectivism were espoused by both Catholic and non-Catholic in the form of a sense that they would be held accountable to God or to some higher Power for their decisions as both persons and as educational leaders. One superintendent of a public school system said,

> When it is all said and done, you have to go beyond the sociological stuff. I believe in divine guidance. People have to have free will but they also have to be held accountable for their actions. Ethical decisions – I think about ultimate accountability. I talk to people about decisions. I ask "what is the right thing" and "what will keep me out of trouble?" Gut instinct is [an] important factor.

Another made a comparable comment when he indicated that,

> The provision of public education is really important and, at the end of the day, the Great One upstairs – he or she or it – will be the judge and I want to know that I was doing something that counted. I think that's what I call Christian humanism. It has had a lot of influence on me.

Finally, religious reflectivism was expressed in the form of personal or individual spiritual pilgrimages. From a Catholic jurisdiction, one superintendent expressed his grounds for the difficult administrative challenges he faced when he said,

> We have a great story related to when Christ was in the boat with his disciples and he was sleeping. The wind was blowing and the waves were coming and everything else and basically – that's where we are right now. I am one of those disciples yelling about all these problems and Christ is there, he is just at the back. All we have to do is pray, all we have to do is believe and Christ will not let us go down. He is not going to let the boat go. He is not going to let humanity totally mess itself up. What we have got to do is – you know Christ woke up and said, "Oh ye people of little faith. Do you think that when I am lying there sleeping I am not thinking about you or protecting you? I am not gone, I am with you. I am with you always." So he calmed the sea and he calmed the wind. That's what is going to happen with all these types of problems. We are people of little faith. And that's

> what we have got to do. There is meaning to this. I am convinced in my own way and in my own self that God gets your attention through adversity.

Another spiritually oriented director expressed his "Faith" grounds for decision-making as follows:

> I believe that my heart really works well. My head says – you stupid fool, you should do this or that . . . but my heart says no, that is not what God's will is today. God gives me enough in my life, enough light for one step. I take the one step and that doesn't mean you don't try to step in a direction here and there, I do that.

It is apparent that religious centered grounds brought solace to some of the educational leaders. Their dependence upon their faith for ethical direction and guidance, combined with certainty, shared responsibility, and the acknowledgement that as the decision makers they too were on a faith journey where errors will occur provided succor for the anxiety felt when making ethical decisions in their positions as educational leaders.

## Natural Principles

While the sources for natural law theories can be either theistic or non-theistic, most natural law theories center on both habits and norms. Aquinas is attributed with having presented a rational process by which a person was said to be able to make proper choices in particular contexts based on their wise interpretation and application of ultimate principles. His version of natural law presented an encouragement to scrutinize: the intrinsic good of an action or a practice; the decision-maker's purity of motive, reason and intent; the proximate and remote consequences likely from the act; and, consideration of the circumstances in which the decision was to be made. These elements must all be present before any decision to act would be deemed right or good. While no one superintendent expressed all four of these elements as his or her grounds for decision-making, each element was considered important by at least some of those interviewed.

Although no quotations are herein provided, the survey data indicate, as aforesaid, that one third of the leaders perceived harm avoidance and honesty as inherently important to ethical decision-making. Further, the sense of half of the leaders was that with power came moral responsibility and hence almost all agreed that being independent to make decisions was necessary in order to act ethically, as they would be responsible for their actions as holders of the public trust. This sense of responsibility extended not only to decision-making but also to providing reparations to those injured as a result of a decision wrongfully taken, or in error, or with unintended hurtful consequences.

Natural law's basic concept suggested that a leader should pursue those goods related to fundamental human inclinations. A balanced realization of these inclinations in the superintendents' work would lead to personal and professional fulfillment. The common principles associated with natural law are the concepts of dignity of the human person, the social character of the person, love, and the essence of human relationships. While the concepts of natural, core, universal or *prima facie* ethical values might be appropriately placed under either deontologism or reflectivism, these have been considered in an earlier ethical frame.

## Commentary on the Reflectivist Frame

Ostensibly, the reflective category cannot be lumped into one assessment as it involves: core character values; *practical wisdom* and the *golden mean*; religion-based criteria; and natural law criteria in ethical decision-making. Nevertheless, all of the above are based upon either the premise that it is from the decision-maker's own life experience (hence habits as suggested by Dewey, 1922; see also Buber, 2002, pp. 132-135) or alternatively from a third party's code or set of behavioural rules that ethical decisions ought to be based. In other words, ethical values are to be determined by the experiences which one has had in life; or, alternatively, by some Archimedean point authority to which one turns over the ultimate responsibility for decision-making. In the former case, the assumption is made that experience and habit best define ethical decision-making, where as the latter resonates with words such as "I was just following orders." In both cases there is the sense that an ethical value is objective, sterile, and ready to be plucked-off of the shelf of experience or from a book, and ready for application in any situation. Reflection is merely thought related to value's applicability or application. What is singularly missing in the respondents' responses is the understanding that essentially, as Buber (1952) said,

> We find the ethical in its purity only there where the human person confronts himself with his own potentiality and distinguishes and decides in this confrontation without asking anything other than what is right and what is wrong in this his own situation. . . . One may call the distinction and decision which arises from these depths the action of the *preconscience.* (p. 125)

In essence, Buber was suggesting that there is an inner awareness in individuals which pre-exits knowledge or experience and which informs the individual of right and wrong, good and bad. This is not the morally autonomous individual suggested by Bauman (1993) who, like Heidegger's solitary individual "stands before himself and nothing else, and – since in the last resort one cannot stand before oneself – he stands in his anxiety and dread before nothing" (Buber, 2002, p. 204), nor Aristotle's "*hexis* . . . which is a tendency or disposition, induced by our habits, to have appropriate feelings" (Kraut, 2001), nor the discovered sense of ethics resulting from education suggested by Plato. Rather, it is the existential existence of the individual on the *narrow ridge* where all of the aforementioned considerations exist but where the individual has the freedom to respond *to* them and *from* within herself or himself. It is the actualization of the self within the temporal flux in the moment of decision, in the concrete circumstances and it is the creation of the ethical moment by that decision which denotes the act as ethical or unethical. It is by that act that the wholeness and presence of the individual is in the "awareness of what he really is, of what in his unique and nonrepeatable created existence he is intended to be" (Buber, 1952, p. 125).

Having looked at the four frames employed by educational leaders in ethical decision-making (see summary in Appendix A) and the critical commentary following each, one is left with the question, "How can one stop dancing and learn to live upon the narrow ridge?" It is to that question that we now turn.

# Living Upon The Narrow Ridge

We began this monograph with a quotation by Martin Buber concerning his concept of the Narrow Ridge where we said that "the individual decision-maker finds that ethical decsion making is not based merely upon what is right or wrong, true of false, but rather decisions are forged within a state of paradox where there is a unity of ostensible opposites." We have taken the reader into the minds of educational decsion-makers who experience that sense of paradox and at times ethical ataxia in order, in part, to answer the concerns,mentioned in the rationale for this monograph, that "we know surprisingly little about contemporary conditions of practice" of educational decsion makers. We have utilized quantitative and qualitative data, and through synthesis and analysis, our findings are grouped within four ethical orientations or frames: teleology (utilitarianism), deontology (duty), relativism, and reflectivism. Those findings were subjected to a further critical analysis by employing Martin Buber's concepts of the *narrow ridge* and his *I-Thou*, *I-It* perspective. Table 1 provides an overview of the journey of this monograph, through the various frames and warrants of ethical decision-making.

**Table 1. A Summary of the Four Frames and Their Warrants for Ethical Decision-making**

| Teleological | Deontological | Relativism | Reflectivism |
|---|---|---|---|
| Best Interests of Kids | Self-evident | Emotions: Personal Preference | Character Centered |
| Securing Educational Goals | Rules of Obligations | Egoism: Self-interest | Wisdom Centered |
| Long Term Interests | Reversibility Principle (Golden Rule) | Cultural Relativism: Community Sentiment | Religion Centered |
| Well Being of Stakeholders | Impartiality and Dignity of Persons | Simple Relativism: Extra rational | Natural Principles |
| | Retrospective Obligations | Context Relativism: Situational | |

What have we concluded about educational decision-making upon the Narrow Ridge? It appears that, as with all things human, there is great complexity as decision makers draw upon all four orientations depending upon the nature of the situation facing them at a particular moment. As intuitively one or more of the orientations seem most appropriate to resolve the situation. This approach presents itself as a kaleidoscope of immediate, short term, and long term concerns within the categories of the personal, professional, institutional, relational, and of course – the ethical. It is also evident that there is a tangible sense of being alone when the cacophony of voices becomes quiet and the time comes to decide. That decision is found to be – unlike those of individuals not in public office, to be both personal and public in nature. In the end, Robert Audi (2007, pp. 119-120) said it well in his pluralistic view of the frames of ethical doctrines and their use in life:

> Each of these ethical views is connected with a theory of value. For virtue ethics, the good is achievement of excellence in thought, action, and character. For Kantian ethics, the dignity of person and, as a central aspect of it, good will, are the most important (though not the only) values; and good will is above all a matter of having governing intentions – those determining one's life plans – that accord with the Categorical Imperative. For classical utilitarianism, pleasure and pain are the basic positive and negative values. For the common-sense intuitionist position there is a rich plurality of values. These include values corresponding to virtue, dignity and enjoyment; but on my view moral value has a special place, and there is no closed list of values. Some are, for instance, distinctively aesthetic, some

> intellectual, some religious and some interpersonal in the way that the values of friendship are. Each of the ethical views can play an important part in facilitating a good life . . . on the pluralistic account of value I have presented, radically different kinds of lives can be good. But all good lives seem to contain, in some proportion, the pleasures of social interaction, the rewards of excellence in what we are best at, the exercise of freedom, the animated use of our higher faculties in activities we like, the sense of human dignity in ourselves and others, and, for some people, spiritual satisfactions, whether specifically religious or not.

We have found that all educational decision makers seek internal and external warrants for their decisions and often are unable to articulate the ethical reasons for those decisions. We conclude that using the Buberian approach in deliberations involving ethical matters offers some clarity to decision makers as they live their professional lives authentically and with integrity upon the Narrow Ridge.

The findings of this research indicate that the respondents did not limit themselves to the use of only one ethical framework. Rather, when faced with either making an ethical decision as the primary decision-maker or when advising their political superiors on what was an ethical decision, they drew on multiple orientations. Depending upon the circumstances, the operant approach for educational leaders seemed to be a proclivity toward one dominant orientation which could be varied or supplemented by other frames; thus, their respective warrants, in particular situations. The result of employing a cafeteria style of ethical frames and warrants plays to the feeling of angst and confusion on the decision-makers which, as one respondent suggested, kept him up late at night in trying to resolve complex ethical issues.

The above is in concert with the earlier findings from the literature that educational leaders feel alone in their ethical decision-making. They find it difficult to articulate their warrants for decisions, and are somewhat reluctant to discuss their intuitive, very personal, meta-analytical approaches to ethical decision-making. Their feelings of discomfort may well be explained by Buber's concepts of the *I-It* and the *I-Thou* relationship. The teleological and deontological frames are effective in a simple sense in arriving at decisions. However, both focus upon the other person or persons as an *it*: that is, a being who is acted upon by the decision maker whose warrant for such action is an end justified outside of the other (the *It*) and the *I*, or justified by a duty which acts with moral force upon the *I* and brute force (in terms of effect or outcome) upon the other. Both have priority over the *I* and the other as persons.

The relativism and reflectivism frames in distinction from the other two frames, are focused primarily on the *I*, which looks inward for the sufficiency of ethical warrant: survival, emotions, habit, sacrosanct texts as interpreted by the *I*. These warrants are essentially *self-referential* and *self-reverential* and although their application may at times provide succor for the decision-maker, the decisions are not tied to the immediate, authentic relational self. Why? For Buber, to be authentic it is necessary to be in relationship, not with the *It* but rather with the other as the responsive, intersubjective *Thou*; asking nothing from *Thou* but the act of relating with another, which is immediate, truthful, and essentially experiential. Without that dialogical, mutual, authentic relationship with the other as *Thou*, one is merely acting mechanically for specific purposes when in relation with others. For Buber the purpose is the *I-Thou* relationship itself, as it is the only way one can be authentic to the human self, in distinction from any sought ends or means. What does this mean to the education leader who must make ethical decisions? We suggest that it means that one must enter into relationship with those who will or may be affected by a decision during its formularization in order to encounter the *Thou* and know him, or her, or them as humans before acting in ways that affect their lives. It is in that dialogical and reciprocal relationship of the *I-Thou* that the decision maker can best understand the nature of the human effects of a decision beyond teleology, deontology, relativism, and reflectivism.

It is suggested that stating that ethics are relative, or that one should do what is best for the majority or looking to the overt results of the act, or looking to rules from society, God, nature, or relying on a professional code, or falling back upon one's duty are not singularly or collectively satisfying recourses for all occasions of decision. As Buber suggested, those orientations are mere mental artifices and hence are not at the center of acting in a purely human sense. The ethical orientations presented here must be interpreted by the individual in their application to specific situations. Leadership and the exercise of ethical leadership are situated. This essentially leaves the educational leader engaged in the moment, with a choice to take full personal responsibility for the decision made and, as a consequence, to create who they will be in the act of decision-making. In that sense, the fundamental ethical question is not the actual decision but rather *the appreciation that one is experiencing an existential moment of becoming who one really is, and to choose to act in an authentically human fashion* having entered into the *I-Thou* relationship. The relationship sought is *I-Thou* and not *I-It*; where other people are not merely means (or "its"). Feeling torn between the various available options of ethical orientations, whether teleological, deontological, relativism or reflectivism, while seeing that many orientations ostensibly and rationally apply to a situation, the decision-maker feels a sense of ataxia and paradox while navigating Buber's narrow ridge.

Buber suggested that it is in the reciprocity of experiential dialogue with the other that moves the other from an *It* to a *Thou* and, in turn, while in this momentary mutuality, in this place of meeting, in the action of reciprocal dialogue, that I am actualized as a human in my wholeness. It is a courageous act of meeting and becoming and it is for the self . . . authentic. This is not the existential aloneness of the I in a closed system existence, as described by Heidegger. Buber (2002) stated,

> The man of real existence in Heidegger's sense, the man of 'self being,' who in

> Heidegger's view is the goal of life, is not the man who really lives with man, but the man who can no longer really live with man., the man who knows real life only in communication with himself. . . . Heidgger islolates from the wholeness of life the realm in which man is related to himself., since he absolutizes the temporally conditioned siituation of the radically solitary man, and wants to derive the essence of human existence from the experience of a nightmare. (pp. 199-200)

It is mutual relationship with another, when that relationship is the *I-Thou*, that one is authentically human, responsible, and free as an ethical being. This is not to say that one must dissolve one's individuality into togetherness. Buber (2004) stated that at this meeting with others you "are to hold your ground when you meet them" (p. 31).

The reader may say, all this is fine but as an administrator, I must justify my actions to others in terms they understand and in ways that will have meaning for them. This is a good point but it mechanistic and misses the key issue which is that the decision-maker must first, and most importantly, be authentic in her or his decision-making in order to have integrity. It is with that sense of integrity, of wholeness in their integrated self, that the decision-maker is best capable of acting ethically as there is no one to shift blame onto: no blame accepting god, code, or society, and nowhere to hide from the existential decision of being authentic to who one is becoming as a result of the act of decision-making. *The important point is that it is the act of decision-making that forms the person, not the framework from which one may choose nor the warrant sought for justification of the decision.*

Standing upon the narrow ridge from where we view the various ethical orientations is not comfortable as we stand alone not in deciding which to choose, but ethically, to act authentically from being *for* the Other in the *I-Thou* relationship. This is the position of the ethical decision-maker and the time in place by which she or he defines the self and the decision as ethical.

With Buber, we suggest that "the idea of responsibility is to be brought back from the province of specialized ethics, of an 'ought' that swings free in the air, into that lived life. Genuine responsibility exists only where there is real responding" (Buber, 2002, p. 18; Taylor, 1992; Starratt, 2003).

This monograph has provided quantitative, qualitative, and analytical findings related to the ethical orientations of a set of superintendents of education. We have clustered those orientations into four categories, relativism, utilitarianism, reflectivism, and deontologism and critiqued each from the viewpoint of Martin Buber's concepts of the *narrow ridge* and his *I-Thou*, *I-It* perspective. We have suggested that by applying Buber's concepts, decision-makers may not only avoid the various criticisms associated with the various doctrines but emerge as an authentic ethical decision-maker.

# Postscript: One Person's Experience with Dancing

The simplest and most mundane of stories and experiences can profoundly shape our ethical lives and cause us to reflect in a fashion that forever leaves and imprint on our lives and the way we live. Denhardt and Denhardt (2006) ask:

> so what is it that leaders do, consciously or unconsciously, that causes others to follow? We think the answer lies not in the leader's providing explanations, but in the leader's connecting with people in a way that energizes them and cause them to act. The leader must touch not only the "head" but also the "heart." The leader must address basic human values and do so in terms of the future. (p. 20)

They say that "to engage in and to respond to this kind of leadership, is to enter into the dance of leadership" (p. 21). What are some of the stories and experiences in your life that have been allowed to make a difference in the way you live and lead? Why not write some of these stories down and pass them along. We have long known that effective and efficacious ethical decision-making is more than an act of the mind (Pascal's view that "the heart has reasons that reasons knows not of" comes to mind). Here is such a story by one of your authors. The story connects to the theme of "dancing on the narrow edge."

*I'd been there with Viv and two good friends, Bev and Dick, a couple of months earlier so I wasn't too disappointed when I received one fewer ticket for the Jay Leno Show in Burbank for my son, Graham and his friend, Mark, than I had requested. I thought maybe I'd see if there were any standby tickets when I dropped them off. I have huge respect for Jay's main guest of the day, Director Ron Howard, but I could also handle two and a half hours in a coffee shop with my backpack of work while I waited for the boys.*

*Dressed like a parent-taxis driver (in my case that was a colourful Hawaiian shirt, brown shoes, black socks, and orange shorts which like the word "orange" wouldn't match anything) I dropped the boys off on Alameda and Olive then went to search for a parking spot. When I finally got back to where the boys had lined up with about a hundred anticipating others I was sweating up a storm – it was hot and the hike from the "no-air conditioning but cheap on gas" car had been a considerable one. I asked one of the guest attendants if there was any chance I might get into the Show on stand-by. He told me that my chances were slim but suggested I ask along the line to see if anyone had an extra. The first group of four I bashfully asked did have an extra; so with ticket in hand I went back to where the boys were standing.*

*It was an hour and a half wait and though we were in the shade, it was a hot, people-watching wait. Once in the studio, we were ushered into excellent seats. We joined the almost 400 other spectators, entering into the fascinating flurry of technical preparations for the nightly show. I spotted the grey pony-tailed "warm-up guy-hippie." I shared my unchecked memories with the boys that spoke poorly of this fellow's behaviour observed during Viv and my earlier attendance. He had consistently put several people down, embarrassed and insulted them while giving the audience tips, directions and pseudo-enthusiasm for the upcoming show. I'd become angry as I'd let his unnecessary and cruel manners get under my skin. I told the boys how I felt, partly to vent and partly to prepare them.*

*As show time approached, it was his turn. It was the same old shtick; he got people laughing (uncomfortably at first) at the poor souls he embarrassed. Then for his final segment he asked for some volunteers to stand as an indication of their interest to come to the stage to dance. I'd forgotten this part from our earlier experience, until he mentioned it. Well of course I did not stand. I would never do so – I am an introvert and I don't dance. I only dance on the "inside" – under normal circumstances you'd only see me dancing if you looked into my eyes on a good day!*

*Well, I was in an aisle seat so I dipped slightly, leaned inward to the boys and tightly drove my butt further into the theatre seat. I whispered a thankful prayer that the selection was apparently going to be from amongst the standing and that there were lots of them to chose from. I sure didn't like the way this man made fun by picking on people. I hated that we, as an audience, found his demeaning behaviour funny – at least when we were not the object of his up close and personal ridicule. He walked up the aisle past me, then he looked back – there was no way he'd be looking me in the eye. My eyes were purposefully no where to be found. But he saw me and told me I was among the chosen. He stood there, impatiently waiting for my reluctant obedience to find legs. Left with a choice between immediate ridicule and eventual embarrassment I chose the later. Up I went with the others – four beautiful young ladies, one full-faced and a smiling 75 year old, and two middle-aged, worse-for-wear guys (including me).*

*We huddled up with a stage manager to receive our instructions. We were to go out onto center stage when tapped on the shoulder, dance to what ever variation of music the sound people played, endure the laughter and applause of the audience then move off when signaled to do so by the hateful hippie when he ran out of nasty things to say and as another "volunteer" was tapped for their performance. It was a temporary relief when I was placed last in line. I looked up at Graham and Mark. They could hardly contain their pleasure – they were clearly enjoying all this more than I was. My tap came and I walked forward. The lights were on me, the audience as clearly laughing at me (I know it wasn't with me) but I made the best of the situation and "danced." To ease my nervousness I verbally observed to the evil man standing a few yards ahead of me that we had on similar Hawaiian shirts. Surely we didn't have similar tastes I thought to myself. I couldn't catch everything he said with the music blaring but I did hear him say something like "that outfit must have looked a lot better on the store mannequin eh!" An eternity or perhaps a few seconds later the bad-mouthed warm-up guy disappeared – abandoning his duty post for waving people off and went behind me to Jay Leno's desk where he began giving the participants Leno loot for their cooperation. Afraid of his reproof for leaving before his signal, I kept on dancing to the music, smiling politely at the couples in the front row who were howling at me and knowing that the boys would be unsympathetically taken with the hilarity of situation. Red-faced, I wondered when this misery would end but on the outside trying to look like I was okay with it all. Finally he waved me "stop" and I left the stage, cheap Jay Leno baseball hat in hand.*

*When I arrived at my seat the boys appeared to have no strength in their bodies, they were gasping for air and had tears of "joy" in their eyes. The rest of the show was relatively uneventful and actually quite enjoyable. By the end, I was sort of glad I had been able to get the ticket. Graham told me the mannequin comment was the highlight of his Jay Leno experience.*

*As we exited the Show, the warm-up guy was walking out right next to me. "End of your work day," I asked him in a friendly-by-faith tone. "Yep," he said reluctantly and with no care, no personal acknowledgement - just as he ducked out through a door for Show Personnel Only. "Not too friendly," Graham commented when we were on our own. "Nope, not very" I replied, but thinking inside how pleased I was that my own flesh and blood saw the flaws in this man's manner – even if it was for different reasons.*

*This week I've been thinking about the difference between servanthood and servitude – I'd experienced servitude in the service of a certain kind of entertainment. Perhaps I'd been the mannequin, an unusually suited one to be sure. And what about the off-duty warm-up actor who I'd try to befriend as his audience was no longer there for him. Was it all a repetitive act before faceless people for him. Was my Hawaiian-shirted twin a mannequin too? Or was he a man with family, friends, and a very different life outside the studio? What would the remainder of his day, his dance, and his relationships look like, I wondered? Then*

*I recalled the "could-have-been-life-long friends" from Wisconsin we'd met in line early.*

*Let me back up a bit. Before I'd arrived from parking the car, Graham had somehow conveyed to these folks that I was a dignified professor and okay father, on sabbatical to Southern California from Canada. When I joined the line, their first question to me had been – "How have you found your time here?" It turned out that they'd left the "insane busyness" of their Southern California experience 17 years earlier to raise their family in rural civility and with the relative calm that the life of a Midwestern couple and a successful lawn implement dealership might afford. I did nothing to dissuade them from the impression that my "from-time-to-time-loyal offspring" had left with them. They added delight to the day and certainly helped the wait in line proceed with unpretentious and engaging conversation. They'd been seated towards the back of the studio, above us by about 10 rows. In fact I would have loved to have had more time with them. I wonder how they saw all of this from their higher view. Indeed what would they think of the rarified professor now? Would they have been laughing or have felt my pain and humiliation? Would they have thought that all of this did me some good? Would they have asked, again, "how have you found your time here?"*

*I read this week that our lives can be likened to a tree: the shadow our reputation; the leaves, branches and trunk our visible personality; and the roots our character. What resemblance is there, shadow to roots, in my life? What good does it do to feed, worry or give deference to one's shadow, as it comes and goes with the moments of the day? Oh for the grace of "inside" dancing every day.*

Our best wishes to you – in your dancing on the narrow ridge.

Keith and Kent, 2010

# Appendix "A"
## Grounds For Ethical Decision-making Questionnaire

In this questionnaire, you will find a series of general statements commonly held opinions for which there are no right or wrong responses. For example, you may agree or strongly agree with some items and disagree or strongly disagree with others. We are interested in the extent to which you agree or disagree with each of these statements. Please consider each item from your perspective as an educational leader (superintendent or assistant superintendent).

PLEASE:

1. Read each statement carefully.
2. Think about the degree to which you think/feel each of the following statements agrees or disagrees with your ethical point of view.
3. Place and X in the O whether you:

DS = Strongly Disagree
D = Disagree
N = Neutral
A = Agree
SA = Strongly Agree

| | | DS | D | N | A | SA |
|---|---|---|---|---|---|---|
| **1.** | **Decisions are right if they promote happiness.** | O | O | O | O | O |
| 2. | The moral views of my school-community determine what is good, right or virtuous. | O | O | O | O | O |
| **3.** | **Ethical decisions result in the greatest good for the greater number.** | O | O | O | O | O |
| 4. | It is natural for people to act in the best interest of others. | O | O | O | O | O |
| **5.** | **What is ethical changes with time and circumstances.** | O | O | O | O | O |

| | | DS | D | N | A | SA |
|---|---|---|---|---|---|---|
| 6. | The fairness of a social norm gives it an ethical force. | O | O | O | O | O |
| **7.** | **Maximizing the short term benefit for ourschool-communities is an ethical imperative for policy-making in education.** | O | O | O | O | O |
| 8. | The rightness of a moral action is always in keeping with one's obligation(s) to a higher Power (i.e., God). | O | O | O | O | O |
| **9.** | **Maximizing the long term benefits for our students and staff is a very important guide for our policy-making.** | O | O | O | O | O |
| 10. | Leaders should always treat people as subjects of value rather than means for accomplishing particular purposes. | O | O | O | O | O |
| **11.** | **The best test of right is whether God or a higher Power would approve.** | O | O | O | O | O |
| 12. | Two attitudes are adequate for the majority of ethical decisions: love God and love your neighbour. | O | O | O | O | O |
| **13.** | **Asking which action of two alternate actions reflects stronger duty is an ethical way to sort out dilemmas.** | O | O | O | O | O |
| 14. | The rightness or wrongness of an action is mainly a function of the consequences that maybe anticipated from that action. | O | O | O | O | O |
| **15.** | **I try to act such that the principle behind my action could become a safe ethical guide for others to follow.** | O | O | O | O | O |
| 16. | Acting against one's own interest is contrary to reason. | O | O | O | O | O |
| **17.** | **We should always treat people as ends, not as means to achieve some ends.** | O | O | O | O | O |
| 18. | One cannot do right without the insight and courage derived from some higher Power. | O | O | O | O | O |
| **19.** | **When making a difficult decision, I ask if the alternative is consistent with the overall welfare of the people in the organization.** | O | O | O | O | O |
| 20. | I believe everyone knows what is essentially right and wrong. | O | O | O | O | O |

| | | DS | D | N | A | SA |
|---|---|---|---|---|---|---|
| **21.** | **Religious codes such as the Ten Commandments and/or the Sermon of the Mount help me make most ethical decisions.** | O | O | O | O | O |
| 22. | My moral philosophy stipulates that I do what is right from God's perspective. | O | O | O | O | O |
| **23.** | **The rightness of an action is best determined by whether the people affected experience happiness or not.** | O | O | O | O | O |
| 24. | Morality is properly understood as a matter of taste not reason. | O | O | O | O | O |
| **25.** | **The reason that honesty is important is because it promotes social harmony and accord.** | O | O | O | O | O |
| 26. | Honesty is an intrinsically good. (always good) | O | O | O | O | O |
| **27.** | **Honesty is a basic human duty.** | O | O | O | O | O |
| 28. | Honesty is situationally dependent. | O | O | O | O | O |
| **29.** | **People should always avoid harming others (either directly or indirectly).** | O | O | O | O | O |
| 30. | A principal should never lie. | O | O | O | O | O |
| **31.** | **Breaking a promise is always an unethical act.** | O | O | O | O | O |
| 32. | The needs of another human being always places those with resources in positions of moral obligation. | O | O | O | O | O |
| **33.** | **Principals need to guard their ability to make independent ethical judgements (i.e.) free from undue influences and conflicts of interest.** | O | O | O | O | O |
| 34. | Leaders are not obligated to accept responsibility for the foreseeable consequences for either their decisions or non-decisions. | O | O | O | O | O |
| **35.** | **Principals must always endeavour to be beyond reproach and avoid even the appearance of impropriety.** | O | O | O | O | O |
| 36. | School principals have a special obligation to respect the democratic processes of decision-making. | O | O | O | O | O |

| | | DS | D | N | A | SA |
|---|---|---|---|---|---|---|
| **37.** | **A person always has a moral responsibility to make reparation for wrongful acts.** | O | O | O | O | O |
| 38. | "It is easier to know what is right than it is to do it". | O | O | O | O | O |
| **39.** | **"It is easier to explain why an ethical choice is right than it is to do what is right".** | O | O | O | O | O |
| 40. | In my view, there are many opportunities for a school principal to behave unethically. | O | O | O | O | O |
| **41.** | **In educational leadership, there is often insufficient time available to consider the ethical implication of tough choices.** | O | O | O | O | O |
| 42. | I believe that successful principals are generally more ethical than unsuccessful principals. | O | O | O | O | O |
| **43.** | **To succeed in my particular jurisdiction, I am sometimes required to compromise my personal views of right and wrong.** | O | O | O | O | O |
| 44. | The optimal choice is that which produces the best social consequences. | O | O | O | O | O |

# Reference List


Ayer, A.J. (1952). *Language, truth, and logic.* New York: Dover Publications Inc.

Audi, R. (2007). *Moral value and diversity.* Oxford: Oxford University Press.

Bauman, Z. (1993). *Postmodern ethics.* Malden, Mass: Blackwell.

Beckner, W. (2003). *Ethics for educational leaders.* Upper Saddle River, NJ: Allyn and Bacon.

Begley, P., & Leonard, P. (Eds.)(1999). *Values in educational administration: A book of readings.* New York: Falmer Press.

Begley, P.(Ed.). (1999). *Values and educational leadership.* New York: SUNY Press.

Bird, F., & Waters, J. (1989). The moral muteness of managers. *California Management Review. 8,* 73-88.

Bird, F., & Waters, J. (1987). The nature of managerial moral standards. *Journal of Business Ethics. 6,* 1-13.

Bottery, M. (1993). *The ethics of educational management.* London: Cassell Educational Limited.

Buber, M. (2002). *Between man and man.* (Trans. R.G.Smith) London: Routledge. [Original published 1947].

Buber, M. (1948). Israel and the world: Essays in a time of crisis. New York: Schocken Books.

Buber, M. (1958). *I and thou (2nd ed.)* Trans. R.G. Smith. New York: Charles Scrbner's Sons.

Buber, M. (1952). *Eclipse of God: Studies in the relation between religion and philosophy.* (Trans. M. S. Friedman, et al.). New York: Harper & Brothers.

Charmaz, K. (2000). Grounded theory: Objectivist and constructivist methods. In N.K. Denzin & Y.S. Lincoln (Eds.), *Handbook of qualitative research (2nd ed.)* (pp. 509-535). Thousand Oaks, CA: Sage.

Denhardt, R., & Denhardt, J. (2006). *The dance of leadership: The art of leading in business, government and society.* Armonk, New York: M.E. Sharpe.

Dewey, J. (1922). *Human nature and conduct: An introduction to social psychology.* New York; Modern Library.

Enns, F. (1981). Some ethical-moral concerns in administration. *The Canadian Administrator. 20*(8), 1-8.

Enomoto, E., & Kramer, B. (2007). *Leading through the quagmire: Ethical foundations, critical methods, and practical applications for school leadership.* Lanham, Maryland: Rowman & Littlefield Education.

Friedman, M. (1960). *Martin Buber: The life of dialogue.* New York: Harper and Row.

Fullan, M. (2003). *The moral imperative of school leadership.* Thousand Oaks, CA: Corwin Press.

Fullan, M. (2001). Leading in a culture of change. San Francisco: Jossey Bass Publishers.

Gronn, P. (1987). Notes on leader watching. In R.J.S. Macpherson (Ed.). *Ways and meanings of research in educational administration.* Armidale: The University of New England.

Jackall, R. (1988). *Moral mazes: The world of corporate managers.* New York: Oxford University Press.

Kowalski, T. (1995). *Keepers of the flame: Contemporary urban superintendents.* Thousand Oaks, CA: Corwin Press, Inc.

Kraut, R. (2001). Aristotle's ethics, *The Stanford Encyclopedia of Philosophy (Summer, 2001 Edition),* Edward N. Zalta (ed.) Retrieved May 20, 2005, from http://plato.stanford.edu/archives/sum2001/entries/aristotle-ethics/

Ladd, J. (1957). *The structure of a moral code: A philosophic analysis ofethical discourse applied to the ethics of the Navaho Indians.* Cambridge: Harvard University Press.

Leithwood, K., & Musella, D. (Eds.) (1991). *Understanding school system administration: Studies of the contemporary chief educational officer*. London: The Falmer Press.

Lennick, D., & Kiel, F. (2005). *Moral intelligence*. Upper Saddle River, N.J.: Pearson Education Inc.

Maxcy, S. (2002). *Ethical school leadership*. Lanham, Maryland: The Scarecrow Press.

Nash, R. (1996). *"Real world" ethics: Frameworks for educators and human services professionals*. New York: Teachers' College Press.

Parsons, R. (2001). *The ethics of professional practice*. Boston: Allyn and Bacon.

Rawls, J (1971). A theory of justice. Cambridge: The Belknap Press of Harvard University Press.

Sergiovanni, T. (1996). *Moral leadership: Getting to the heart of school improvement*. San Francisco: Jossey Bass Publishers.

Starratt, R. (2004). *Ethical leadership*. San Francisco: Jossey Bass Publishers.

Starratt, R. (2003). *Centering educational administration: Cultivating meaning, community, responsibility*. New York: Laurence Erlbaum Associates.

Starratt, R. (1994). *Building an ethical school: A practical response to the moral crisis in schools*. New York: Falmer Press.

Schulte, J., & Cochrane, D. (1995). *Ethics in school counselling*. New York: Teachers College Press.

Shakotko, D., & Walker, K. (1999). Poietic leadership. P. Begley & P. Leonard (Eds.). *The Values of Educational Administration* (pp. 201-222). London: The Falmers Press.

Strike, K., Haller, E., & Soltis, J. (1988). *The ethics of school administration*. New York: Teachers College Press.

Strike, K., & Soltis, J. (1985). *The ethics of teaching*. New York: Teachers College Press.

Taylor, C. (1992). *The ethics of authenticity*. Cambridge: Harvard University Press.

Toffler, B. L. (1986). *Tough choices: Managers talk ethics*. New York: John Wiley and Sons.

Walker, K., & Donlevy, K. (2009). The four ethical commitments in educational administration. *Journal of Educational Thought*.

Walker, K., & Sackney, L. (2007). Anti-egoistic school leadership: Ecologically-based value perspectives for the 21st century. In D.N. Aspin & J.D. Chapman (Eds.) *Values Education and Lifelong Learning* (pp. 255-278), New York: Springer Press.

Walker, K., & Donlevy, K. (2006). Beyond relativism to ethical decision-making. *Journal of School Leadership 16*(3), 216-239.

Walker, K., & Shakotko, D. (1999). The Canadian superintendency: Value-based challenges and pressures. P. Begley (Ed.). *Values and Educational Leadership* (pp. 289-313). New York: State University of New York.

Walker, K. (1995a). Influences on the value mediating work of educational leaders. In S. Natale and B. Rothschild (Vol. 28 Eds.). *Work Values: Education, Organization and Religious Inquiry Series* (pp. 213-237). Media, PA: Rodopi Press.

Walker, K. (1995b, September). Perceptions of ethical problems among senior educational leaders. *Journal of School Leadership 2* (6).

Walker, K. (1994). Notions of "ethical" among senior educational leaders. *The Alberta Journal of Educational Research*, XL (1), 21-34.

Zubay, B., & Soltis, J. (2005). *Creating the ethical school: A book of case studies.* New York: Teachers College Press.

## Dr. J. Kent Donlevy (Associate Professor)

B.A., B.Ed., M.Ed., J.D., Ph.D.

Dr. Donlevy works in the Graduate Division of Educational Research in the Faculty of Education at the University of Calgary. He has taught grades 4-12 (inclusive), been a school principal, and is permanently certified as a teacher in both Alberta and Saskatchewan. He has negotiated on local levels for both the Alberta Teachers' Association and the Saskatchewan Teachers' Federation. He is also a member of the Saskatchewan Law Society, having become a barrister & solicitor in 1985.

**His contact information is as follows:**


Graduate Division of Educational Research

Faculty of Education

University of Calgary

2500 University Drive NW

Calgary, Alberta

T2N 1N4

E-mail: donlevy@ucalgary.ca

Tel: 1.403.220-2973

Fax: 1.403.282-3005

## Dr. Keith D. Walker (Professor)

B.P.E (U. of Alberta), B.Ed., M.Ed., Ph.D. (U. of Saskatchewan), Dip.Christian Studies (Regent College), D.D. (honoris causa).

Dr. Walker has worked as a manager, teacher, administrator, minister, and professor in public, private, and non profit sectors for over 3 decades. For the past 18 years Dr. Walker has been a research professor with the Department of Educational Administration and the Johnson Shoyama Graduate School of Public Policy at the University of Saskatchewan. His current work focuses on leadership and governance, organizational development and effectiveness and professional ethics.

**His contact information is as follows:**

Department of Educational Administration/Johnson Shoyama Graduate School of Public Policy

University of Saskatchewan

28 Campus Drive

Saskatoon, Saskatchewan

S7N 0X1

E-mail: keith.walker@usask.ca

Tel: 1.306.966.7623

Fax: 1.306.966.7020

## REVIEWERS' COMMENTS

A draft of this monograph was provided to several academics and senior educational leaders. We sought their critical commentary and suggestions for improvement and this monograph reflects our grateful acceptance of their excellent assistance.

Below are a few of their endorsing comments (we've attempted to revise according to their criticisms and maintain the energy of their commendations).

**Reviewer #1** (University professor and former Chief Superintendent of Education)

The monograph provides a common language and a frame of reference for educational leaders to discuss and make meaning of their experiences with ethical decision-making. You emphasize that it is the act of decision-making that forms the person not the framework they may choose. This, to me is the crux of your monograph.

**Reviewer #2** (University professor and former Associate Dean of Education)

You have brought the reader nicely and logically into the deduction that "… it is the act of decision-making that forms the person, not the framework from which one may choose nor the warrant sought for justification of the decision (p. 53)."

**Reviewer #3** (University professor and former Chief Superintendent of Education)

We should be teaching our administrators more about the language of morals and analyzing from the field moral conundra and 'critical incidents'. I laud the excellence of your work.

**Reviewer #4** (University professor and former Chief Superintendent of Education)

This monograph will . . . provide an opportunity for superintendents to make informed decisions. [It] exposes the lonely world of the superintendent in the decision-making arena. It also provides a forum through which superintendents can consider or reflect on the rationale that they use to make decisions.

81703826R00078

Made in the USA
Middletown, DE
26 July 2018